Make an Egg Card

Catherine Baker
Lisa Austin

Contents

An Egg Card

You can make an egg card.

pens
scissors
pins
tape

Make the Chick

1. Cut out a big circle.

2. Cut out a little circle.

3. Put the little circle on top of the big circle.

4 Put on an eye.

5 Put on a tail.

6 Put on a beak.

Make the Egg

1 Cut out a big egg.

2 Cut a zig-zag in the egg.

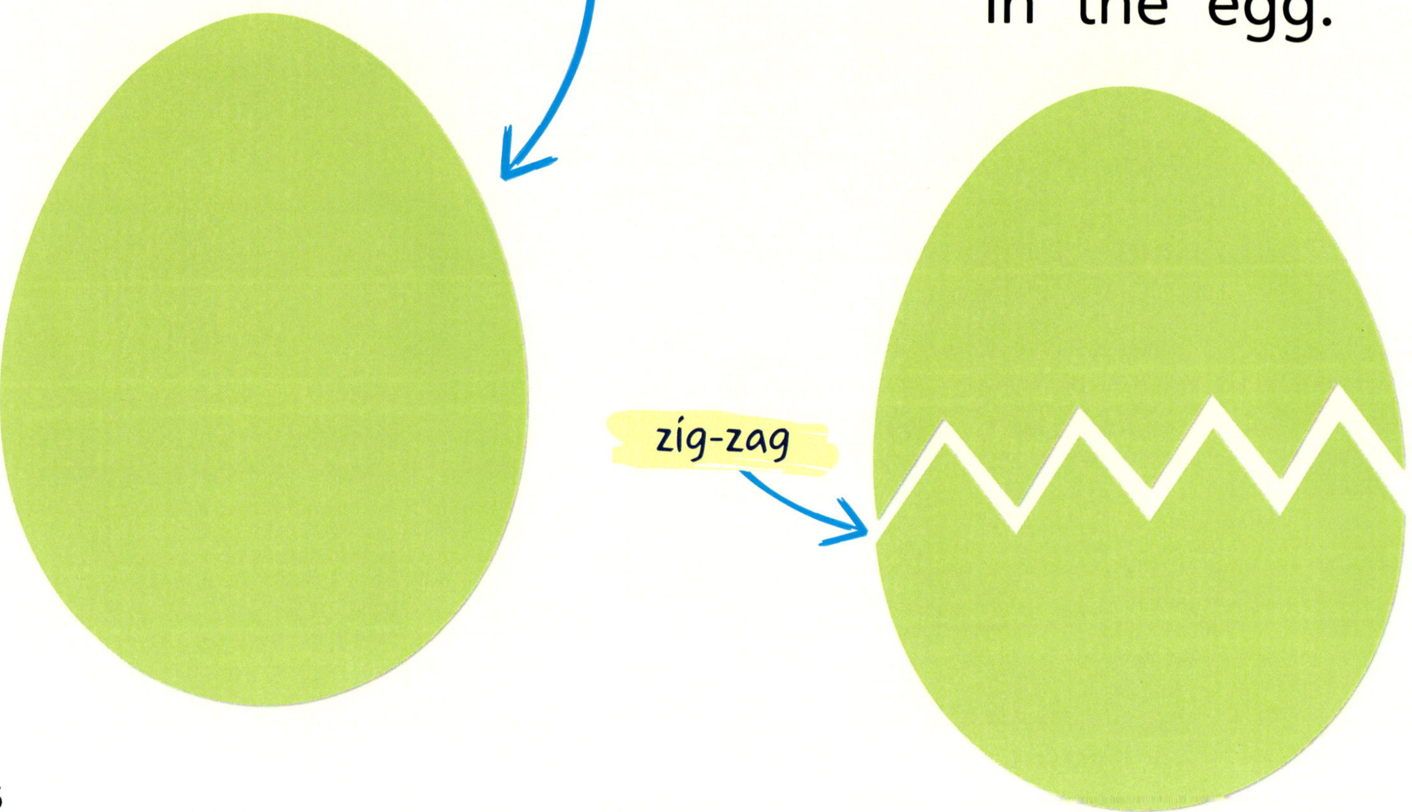

Draw on the Egg

Draw on the top of the egg with your pens.

Pin the Egg

1 Put a pin in the egg.

2 See! You can open and shut the egg.

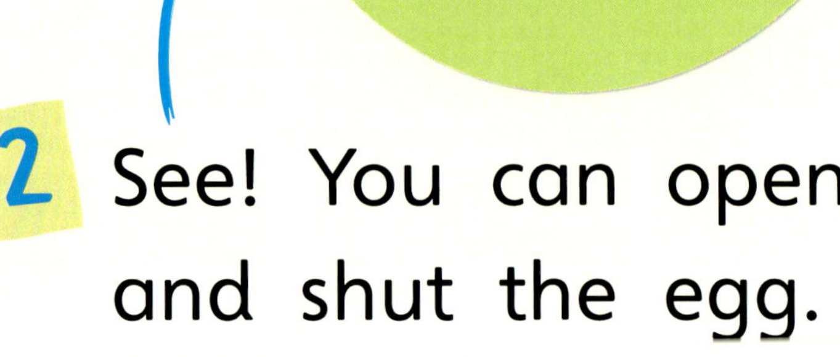

Put the Chick in the Egg

1 Put tape under the chick.

2 Put the chick in the egg.

3 Shut the egg.

On the Card

Put *To Mum* or *To Dad* on the card.
Or, put *To my friend*, on the card.

To Mum

The Egg Card

Give your egg card to Mum, Dad, or a friend!

Cheep! Cheep!